JOURNEY OF THE BROKEN

SAVED BY GRACE

KATHY BOECKMAN

WESTBOW
P R E S S®
A DIVISION OF THOMAS NELSON
& ZONDERVAN

WestBow Press books may be ordered through booksellers or by contacting:

WestBow Press
A Division of Thomas Nelson & Zondervan
1663 Liberty Drive
Bloomington, IN 47403
www.westbowpress.com
844-714-3454

Requests for information should be sent to:
House of Healing, Inc.
7300 Britton Road NE
El Reno, Oklahoma 73936
www.house-of-healing.org

ISBN: 978-1-6642-2622-7 (sc)
ISBN: 978-1-6642-2621-0 (hc)
ISBN: 978-1-6642-2623-4 (e)

Library of Congress Control Number: 2021904516

Print information available on the last page.

WestBow Press rev. date: 4/2/2021

CONTENTS

FOREWORD

I first heard Kathy Boeckman share the story of House of Healing at a women's retreat in Eastern Oklahoma. It was a story birthed from her own life experience, a simple story of a life rescued and later a life that would courageously step into a calling, offering hope to those who needed it. Through Kathy's eyes, those who needed this hope were young at-risk teenage girls.

This was something I understood well. It was crystal clear to me. My life, too, had been profoundly affected by the people God had placed around me during my tender teenage years. I was a good kid but a very lost kid. My darkness was hidden; I was hungry for approval and sought it. My goals were empty and shallow as I looked to the fleeting pleasures of this world to find some sort of fulfillment ... even if it was only temporary. I struggled with insecurity and knowing my purpose. I had parents who loved me, but the influence of the world was greater.

In my freshman year of high school, God placed a strong Christian family in my life to point me toward Christ. They helped me find the firm foundation that would change my life forever; they showed me hope through a life lived with God. If not for the intervention of that family in my life, I would have stayed on a dangerous path that could have led to devastating consequences. Yet the foundation I found through time spent with godly adults changed my life forever.

That night at the women's retreat, as I introduced myself to Kathy, I felt in my heart that we could be truly effective working together … but exactly what that would look like was not yet clear.

Four years later, I heard Kathy share again in a Sunday morning class, this time with an even more fervent passion. My heart was stirred once again, and I knew I had to arrange a meeting. I was a young mom of a baby and a toddler and felt limited as to what I could do to help this incredible ministry, but I knew I wanted to be a part of what God was doing.

Before we met, God put it on Kathy's heart that I should serve on the House of Healing board of directors, and that was just the beginning of my six years of service at House of Healing. Eventually, I had the immense honor of serving as the program director for a mentor program Kathy and I developed.

During those years, House of Healing's address was our own kitchen tables, where we shared countless smiles, laughs, tears, and deep conversations with teenage girls we were honored to serve. Some girls stayed weekends with us or we'd get to attend a fun concert together. There were many days when I would run errands with a teen girl in my front seat. We lived life with these girls and their families, and because of the time spent with them, we saw transformation.

The power of a safe adult investing in a teenage girl is profound. The surmounting pressure teen girls face during these years ought to make the strongest individual take pause. Peer pressure and an insatiable desire for acceptance often leads to drug abuse, alcoholism, and sexual activity, which often leads to anxiety, depression, self-harm, and suicide. The need for young women to understand the truth about who they are is dire; their very lives are at stake.

I remember a sunny Tuesday in the spring of 2012. Kathy called me to meet her in the parking lot of a grocery store to give me some supplies for an upcoming event. My tall, strong friend who rides horses and Harleys had tears in her eyes. She had just dropped off a girl she was mentoring, but it wasn't the girl's home, for home was not an option for her, and this place was even less safe. It was too much for Kathy, her heart spilling over with compassion. I was honored to be there for her to cry and share her heart with, and I was thankful she knew she was not the only one in this world who wanted to *do* something to bring *hope and healing* to teenage girls.

I know we are not alone. Many who read this will nod their heads in agreement because they have a sister, daughter, cousin, or friend who needs the kind of help the House of Healing provides. Many of them *were* this girl … or *are* that girl right now. Hear me when I say that *there is hope.*

As you read this book and the story unfolds of God reaching into Kathy's life, consider that He also wants to reach down into your life. He is calling your name; He is the only hope, and He is our rescuer. He takes our brokenness and makes beautiful things. There is forgiveness for those who turn to him and a new life. There is freedom and a firm foundation. He is our rock.

I ask you, dear reader, to consider the profound gift of life that God offers through His Son Jesus Christ. There is eternal security in a life found in Christ, and it starts the moment you say yes to Him. At House of Healing, we always explain to the girls that their worth is proven in the picture of the cross— their lives were worth dying for, and through that death, the new life given to us is filled with *purpose.*

For we are God's handiwork, created in Christ Jesus to do the good works, which God prepared in advance for us to do.
—Ephesians 2:10

As you read these pages, I hope and pray you will let the redemptive story unfold before you and let it change you. Search your heart and ask yourself if the hope of Jesus is yours, and if so, please share it. If you realize you don't know the hope of Jesus, please reach out using the contact info for the House of Healing. I encourage you to consider supporting the House of Healing so that the work God began in Kathy Boeckman so many years ago may continue.

Paula Cummings
Board member 2011–2016
House of Healing program director 2014–2016

HEATHER MCANEAR, KATHY, PAULA CUMMINGS

You may run across a person with zeal for people in need—but not very often do you find a person with the vision and the commitment to do the hard work over time to bring the vision into a reality. It's hard to face the pain and trauma of your past and allow God to heal wounds. It's hard to humble yourself and reveal to others your painful past so that you can earn their trust. Kathy has proven time and time again that she is tough enough to handle whatever life throws her way and tough enough to trust God to use it all for good in her life and in the lives of teenage girls at risk. May Kathy's story be put into the hands of those who need to hear it most and may they be drawn to the Savior, whom Kathy knows and serves.
—Nancy McKinney

In looking back over 2019 at House of Healing, I am in awe of the way God has worked through our program and the girls. As a volunteer, I feel privileged to be part of such a life-changing ministry. I have witnessed growth through the girls as well as improvements with building plans and expansion. It takes lots of people to make a ministry like the House of Healing grow and move forward. The spring and fall sessions, the retreat, and the monthly Friday night hangouts were a huge success with the girls! I saw relationships being built as well as bonds being made. Not only have the girls learned to work together and build trust, but the mentors did as well. My granddaughter, Kylee, has participated in Authentic Girl and the Equine Experience, and she has taken the things she learned and grown in her confidence and her understanding of God and His love for her. God is definitely working through this ministry. Thank you to everyone who supports the House of Healing.
—Kathy Hill
House of Healing volunteer

CHAPTER ONE

My Humble Beginnings

The memories roll in one by one—some terrible, others beautiful—coming together to create the picture of my past. I see the image forming in my mind. It looks like broken glass, colored glass, stained glass. Glass that was crushed but put back together to create something beautiful. This resembles so much of my life. My memories. They come to me one at a time, a look back at the years gone by, making me the woman I am today.

The memories … Some are crystal clear; others are fuzzy at first. These moments created days, which became decades. Those years made up my stained glass story. The chapters contain brokenness and fragments, yet if I step back and take it all in, it is stunning. It's broken and painful yet beautiful because this story was written by someone bigger than I. I was running, hurting, and self-medicating, while He was working, providing, and bringing me to a future filled with beauty and hope. But let me start with the memories, those mental images from years gone by.

I was born one cold February day in 1961 to Phyllis Ann and

Edward Garnet (he liked to be called Garnet), the youngest of five, like steps on a staircase: Randy, Pam, Debbie, Garnette, and me. Their marriage only survived my first two years. Life was hard. Mama was trying to care for all of us and herself, and she just could not make ends meet. She was a hard worker, waiting tables to keep our heads above water, but she and my dad split up and five kids was a big load to bear. Home was in a small town in Oklahoma. I remember the post office, grocery store, and Main Street. We would drive on back roads, dirt roads, and any ole road that would get us from here to there.

GARNET, PHYLLIS, AND KATHY

I see a strong and beautiful woman, my grandma Fannie Mae Stass. She was small in stature yet big in faith. With the loss of her first husband before I was born, life had not been easy for her. She married Ernie Stass, and they made a life together. She took me in when Mama couldn't raise us any longer. The five of us kids scattered to different homes, and she was my safe place, along with my sister Garnette, my childhood best friend, roommate, playmate—so many pieces of my past include Garnette's face.

Only four days shy of being exactly one year apart, we were almost the same size, often mistaken for twins. Both of us had blonde hair and blue eyes, but my defining feature was the dimples in both cheeks. I can see so clearly two little girls running across the backyard, which seemed to stretch out for miles. My head leaned back, wispy blonde hair blowing in the wind, and I was laughing loudly and feeling carefree. I was running into the playhouse Grandma got for us (kind of like an old storage building), our security, our special place to play and be kids, young and free.

KATHY AND GARNETTE

It's funny which memories our brain chooses to store, while others we can't recall. Like the day I bit Garnette while we were playing outside. I was crying so hard as I raced across the yard, knowing I was in big trouble. But when we got to the house, because of my tears, Grandma assumed *she* bit *me* and spanked Garnette instead ... Oh, but I got my turn when she realized what really happened!

My mind cannot reach further than these years. I don't remember the details, only stories I've heard of what brought us here. Daddy's mom and siblings would come to rescue us kids, until the day finally came when they felt we needed safe and stable places to live, and that's when we were all split up. Garnette and I were with Fannie Mae; I was around two years old and taken out of one home to another. But even though my homelife was interrupted, my memories from this time are as warm and bright as the sunshine on our faces. There were days spent running, laughing, playing— the kinds of stories you expect from a happy childhood—and as I look back, I'm thankful for that time of safety before the storm.

Grandpa Ernie always had a surprise candy in his shirt pocket if I could get his boots pulled off after a long workday. I remember fussing with Garnette over which of us got to try to pull those work boots off. Grandma cleaned the First United Methodist Church, and I remember going to work with her and wiping the wooden pews with wood cleaner. That was my job, and I took pride in it, but I was also just a kid. I recall running in the church and then getting in trouble because this was "God's house" and we were to be respectful inside. Life was simpler back then, growing up in the 1960s. There was no expensive technology or devices to distract us—we were just kids playing outside until the streetlights came on, then making a beeline home as fast as our little legs would carry us.

Home. I think again of Grandma Fannie Mae's house. I see the room I shared with Garnette. Nothing fancy, nothing big. Money was scarce, but it was safe and warm. Above my bed was a painting of a man with kind and loving eyes looking up toward heaven. He had brown hair and a beard. Above his head was a light, almost like a glowing halo, and he was kneeling by a large rock in a place that looked like a garden. Grandma said his name was Jesus and He loved me. That image was the last thing I saw many nights as I drifted off to sleep, and it always filled me with peace. I remember kneeling beside my bed each night, my grandma always praying for me, always thanking God. That woman planted seeds of hope in my heart that didn't take root for many years, but I know this was the beginning of a road that eventually led to faith.

Garnette and I lived with our grandma for about three years and then spent most of our summers at her house after that. Debbie and Pam were living with Aunt Geraldine and Uncle Gene. Aunt Geraldine would bring them to visit us at Grandma's house whenever she could, and we would swing outside and eat watermelon on warm summer days. One evening I stood crying at the window when I had to go inside while everyone else stayed up; being the baby had its downsides. Daddy would come visit us when his job as a long-distance truck driver would allow.

When I was five years old, Grandma lost her second husband, Grandpa Ernie. This was around the same time that Mama was ready to take care of us. She was still waiting tables at Hensley's restaurant, trying as best as she could to take care of our family.

Mom would take us with her mom, Grandma Owen, to Mississippi to visit family. I remember those rides so well. As the littlest, I would have to lie in the back window of the car to give the other kids room in the back seat. I know it's hard to imagine because a child lying in the space under the back widow of the car is illegal today, but my special place to ride had sun on my face and a view. Of course, as the baby, I just wanted a seat by the others.

Grandma Owen's favorite place to stop on road trips was Stucky's, which was a gas station with a huge store inside where we could buy treats and drinks—and we always got a sack of candy.

I was blessed in my childhood to have sweet, loving memories with my grandparents on both sides of the family. There is something special about them, always good to us kids and always fun. Grandpa Owen loved his babies and wanted us to know that; he made sure we had shoes and coats to wear. Unfortunately, both of my grandpas passed away when I was young, but I know that as caring and compassionate men, they had a positive influence on me. Having some healthy men in my life would prove to be so important as I remember what happened next in my story.

My mama married again when I was five years old. The year was 1966, and his name was Roy. Her decision changed everything. The golds and yellows that had made up my childhood so far turned quickly to darker shades in my stained glass story.

CHAPTER TWO

My Broken Childhood

Mama started dating Roy when I was around the age of four. I see my mother in my mind: a beautiful well-kept woman looking her best, with clothes starched and ironed perfectly. She was waiting tables at Hensley's when she met Roy. He was over six feet tall, strong in stature, and stronger in personality, typical for men in his line of work, which was on the Rock Island Railroad. By the time I was five years old, they were getting married and we were moving back in with her and our new stepdad.

It's hard to describe the difficult emotions that came with this season of my life. I was a young girl living a good life with my grandparents and Garnette, who was my best friend in the whole world. My life was fun and free, like childhood should feel, but that didn't change the fact that our other three siblings weren't living with us. It didn't change the fact that our mama hadn't been able to raise us or that daddy was on the road most of the time. I may not have known exactly what I felt, but I wanted all of us to be a family again … and this was our chance!

With my heart full of hopes and dreams for family togetherness, we were back under one roof with mama and Roy. I was five, Garnette six, Debbie nine, Pam ten, and Randy eleven; all seemed right with the world. We were a happy family, like the ones I had heard about in books. We ate dinner together, went out for ice cream, and went to church together every Sunday (something new). Church was a part of Roy's life, and it became a part of ours.

My mom worked all day; Roy worked nights and slept during the day. As the kids, it was our job to have meals ready when she got home and he got up. Debbie and Pam cooked; Garnette and I set the table and did the dishes. We prayed before every meal, and we did not leave the table until everyone was finished. We asked to be excused. Saturday was our cleaning day. We scrubbed and swept the two-story house from top to bottom. I can remember cleaning the bathroom, but it seemed it never was clean enough. I would be sent back at least two or three times to scrub some more. Even though we did not love the chores, I assumed this was what "normal family life" felt like—and it felt great … at first.

When we went to church, it seemed that Roy was an especially important man. People knew him there, and he had a position of leadership, called a deacon. At the time, I did not know or understand what a deacon was, but I later learned the significance. A church has a pastor and other staff positions, also selecting men from the congregation to help the pastor make important decisions. The Bible has a lot to say about the qualities important for someone who is in leadership, and it even lists specific character traits for deacons and elders. The older I became, the more tragic it was to me that the church held some men in such high esteem, yet at home their actions did not match the godliness they were supposed to be filled with. Of course, as a five-year-old girl, none of this was clear to me.

Some memories stick out in my mind like warning signs, screaming to my little heart that things weren't really as good as they seemed. For instance, shortly after we were all back together again, my brother, Randy, moved in with my uncle John. Roy had no mercy on Randy with his discipline, and that is when my uncle took Randy to live with him.

Even memories of our days in church with Roy are tainted with evidence of his anger. Roy sang in the choir, so he was on the stage behind the preacher each week for the entire church service. He made us sit at the front of the church so he could watch us during the sermon, making sure we didn't make a peep or step out of line. I can't even count how many times he came down out of the choir and grabbed one of us by the ear, taking us outside to unleash his anger on our bottom. What puzzles me now is that nobody seemed to think anything was wrong with a furious red-faced man flying down out of the choir loft and grabbing a child with the intention of a harsh spanking. Maybe it was the way parents behaved in that era, maybe they trusted that Roy had self-control and wasn't as angry as he looked, maybe they didn't want to interfere. Regardless of what everyone else was thinking, I was scared stiff.

I remember being so frightened one Sunday when I needed to use the bathroom but knew better than to move a muscle. I ended up having an accident right there at the front of the church, so embarrassed when the other kids made fun of me, then heartbroken when I still got whipped by Roy for having an accident. That memory gives words to describe the atmosphere in our home, an overall feeling of fear and confusion.

Not long after they married, my mama was able to go back to school. She had always wanted to be an LPN, and now she was able to work to become a nurse. Along with going to nursing schools, she kept her job at the restaurant to bring in extra money.

As I've gotten older, I realize that she also kept her job to stay away from home. Not so much to stay away from us but from her new husband, who came with more baggage than she was prepared for. He had had three children of his own, and the blending of our two families turned sour quickly.

Roy's sons, Tommie and Ronnie, were both away serving in Vietnam, but his daughter Barbara came to live with us. Shortly after, Ronnie was shot in the leg and came home on medical leave.

BARBARA, DEBBIE, PAM, KATHY, AND GARNETTE

The relationship between stepchildren and stepparents is a tricky one, with emotions that I'm sure no one really knows what to do with; and as it turned out, Mama and Barbara did not get along and Roy treated us terribly. This created tension and turmoil in the home right away. Barbara did not stay with us long, but we were stuck with Roy, and it must have killed Mama to see him treat us so badly. She knew he whipped us and expected us to be perfect, and I imagine she was afraid to stand up against a man like him. The physical and emotional turmoil began simmering in my soul, but there were other things going on that I had no words or understanding for. There is no excuse; an innocent child should never be put in situations like Roy put me in.

I remember him sitting in the recliner—*"his* recliner," as he liked to remind us. He would be smoking a pipe and watching *Star Trek*. This new man in our life was so strange. He was not like my dad, grandpas, or uncles; and I tried to understand him. When we were at home, he only wore boxer shorts, and often they would gape open while he sat in his chair. I knew it wasn't normal to be wearing only your underwear in public, especially when your private parts were showing, but Roy made Garnette and me sit in the room with him as he watched TV, acting as if he didn't know he was exposing himself to us. I knew it was wrong, felt the ickiness in the pit of my stomach, but he was an adult, my authority figure, and he made us stay. He wanted us to see him like that. This new homelife was not at all what I expected, and it left me confused.

My confusion grew as his behavior became more inappropriate and abusive. Roy began taking me on camping trips to Cedar Lake, and he would let me sit on his lap and drive the truck. He told me it was important for me to learn to drive, but the truth was that he wanted a reason for me to sit on his lap. It felt completely wrong, but he would tell me I needed to learn how to drive with distractions. I knew that the places your bathing suit covers up are off limits, but Roy was an authority figure; I was so confused. *Is this how daddies treat little girls? Do all men behave this way?* It felt wrong in the pit of my stomach, but the behavior continued and he told me I was special.

As his desire grew stronger, taking drives together was not enough. Mama started getting sick often, needing to be hospitalized for periods of time. When she was gone, Roy would make me sleep in bed with him, where he would take advantage of me. A fog of confusion clouded my mind. Roy would have his way with me, saying, "This is our little secret, just between us … and you know you like it too." I was trapped, and my innocence was stolen. My sweet childlike personality became shut down, angry, and people-pleasing.

I was only in elementary school, when I should have been playing with dolls; my greatest care in the world should have been whether we could have ice cream after dinner. Instead, I was holding an enormous amount of secrecy and shame locked tight in my tiny heart.

Running became my stress reliever, and I ran *everywhere*. I brought home many blue ribbons from track at Lincoln Elementary School, in the 100-yard dash and the 220. Around that same time, I found that I could take my frustrations out by smashing a softball— and I loved it! It is tragic to me when I realize that the coaches, players, and other parents only saw a star athlete, never guessing that pain was fueling the success on the track and field … but how would they have known? I didn't tell anyone what went on behind closed doors; I didn't think I could or should. *Was it my fault? Did I do something to make Roy touch me like that? Do all stepdads and daughters have these secrets?* All the questions and secrets were just sitting on my soul like steam in a pressure-cooker, ready to go off.

Hiding became a regular escape. I built a treehouse in the huge old oak tree in our backyard and spent as much time as possible up there. That tree was my safety, the place where I was in control. As long as I was hiding up there, Roy couldn't touch me. I was growing up too quickly, and there was nowhere to go but further into darkness.

As I think back on this time in life, I wish so much to go back and hold that little girl. I wish someone had been there to stand up for me. I wish Mama and the church leaders had stepped in to confront the abusive man who had moved into my life and stolen the little girl that I was.

For that young girl, each new day brought more tears and deeper pain. When you are twelve years old, life is supposed to be a world filled with dreams and wonder, and that should *never* be taken away. My mind was poisoned and tormented, filled with fear instead of the types of anticipation and dreams other girls had: *Who will I marry when I grow up and what will my family be like? Will I get to travel? What will I get to do and see?* Instead, I was haunted by R-rated images and fear. It wasn't fair. Abuse never is.

A heart that can dream and wonder is a *healthy* and *innocent* heart. Yet when you've been pierced with deep pain, your innocence and all dreams for the future are lost. A destructive cycle is then born—pain can quickly turn to anger, and anger finds a way to create more pain. Life becomes a dark place that chokes away the joy of the heart.

I wish I could talk to that girl today, but I can't. I wish I could hold her face in my hands and explain to her that the soft, tender feeling that surprises her sometimes is *God* ... He is reaching out to her with His love; listen to Him and trust Him.

I wish I could tell her to stop believing the lies that spring up from her pain; it's not her fault. She needs to know that her life *does* have purpose and meaning. If she could only have understand how beautiful she truly was ... However, it would be another ten years before she would break free from her nightmare and the memories of sexual abuse.

So many things I wish, yet that was not my reality. I know it never does any good to sit in feelings of regret for the past. The best I can do is acknowledge the injustice and the tragic events that made up my childhood and move forward with the truth that God can (and *did*) use even a traumatic past to bring about a beautiful future.

CHAPTER THREE

My Rebellion and Escape

As the pressure built inside my soul, so did the desire to escape and let off some steam. We had a large pine tree in the front yard. I would climb up to the very top; I could see everything from up there. I felt brave and safe. From high above the ground, I began shooting out the streetlight with my BB gun. This was the first real sign of the storm of rebellion brewing below. It felt good to do something I knew I shouldn't do. Instead of things being done to me, it was my choice, and no one could stop me. I could do what I wanted. There was a new sense of power within me, and I liked how it felt.

When I was in the seventh grade, I began to act out and get into trouble. Debbie and Pam were older than I, so they had jobs and worked all the time. My goal was to stay hidden and not get into big trouble or be noticed and abused. The rebellion in my spirit stayed somewhat shoved down until I discovered smoking and drinking alcohol. Once I had a taste of wine, I was all in, smoking, drinking, and running away from home.

Around this time, I was twelve years old and moved in with my biological dad. I thought moving would be a better situation than living with mom and Roy but quickly learned that life was tough, even in a new house. My dad had a drinking problem, was gone all the time, and I did not have an opportunity to build a relationship with him. Although I was no longer living with Roy's abuse, the climate in Dad's house was toxic as well. When he would come home at night, there was a lot of cussing and physical abuse. With physical, verbal, and sexual violence in my history, I had no idea how to get along or communicate with others in healthy ways.

One evening when I wanted to go out with Debbie, I rebelled against the "no," and a belt came out. I was not about to take another whipping from anyone, so I took that belt and turned it the other way. I obviously thought I would be disciplined, but my dad just laughed and told me not to do that again. That fueled his frustration toward me, and our relationship was destined for disaster. The more he tried to be in control, the more I bucked up to him until he had enough and kicked me out. Bouncing like a pinball, I moved back in with Mom and Roy.

At the age of fourteen, something happened to take the lid off the cooker; all the pressure came rushing out. Mama's husband died of lung cancer. Roy, the one who had used and abused me, stolen my innocence, and made my soul feel like it was dying, was finally gone and never able to hurt me again. I could have my life back, without running and hiding. It seemed as if my heart should feel lighter and relieved, but what my young soul didn't realize was that once abused, the trauma and pain run deeper than one could imagine, and without help, I would continue to self-medicate so I wouldn't feel the pain inside. In celebration of Roy being permanently out of my life, I went out and got drunk.

Roy's passing was the beginning of my behavior getting out of control. It was a downward spiral of smoking pot, huffing spray paint, and running the streets. It was as if Roy's death started a new chapter for all of us, no one knowing how to handle the feelings that come with losing someone who had made such a painful mark on you. We went into survival mode to numb the pain, spending our days with distractions.

I remember one of those days very well. I ran away from home with my best friend. We hopped a train from El Reno to Yukon, the next big town over—maybe fifteen miles away. Looking back, I know God protected us that night from so many things that could have happened.

It was late, and we were walking through a neighborhood. We saw two bicycles lying in a front yard and decided to take them. This was a foolish idea, of course, and what we didn't know was that the parents were sleeping with their bedroom window open, heard us outside, and called the police. We didn't get far riding on our "new" wheels before the police found us. They put us in the police car to take us back to El Reno, but when we came to a stoplight, we both bailed out of the car and ran like crazy—not getting far until we were caught again. This time the police were not soft on us; we were handcuffed and shackled, taken to the police department, and put in a jail cell to scare us.

That it did for me! I just wanted out of there. I can still remember that terrible night in the cold, dark all-cement cell—I knew I didn't want any part of that ever again. At the jail, they called Mom to come get me, but she would not. So the next option was my sister Debbie, and she drove over to get me.

After that experience, I began living with Debbie, and her husband Sam. They did not have money to feed themselves, so taking on another person was a huge financial strain, and they weren't getting any additional help to support me. Debbie was always so good to me and didn't make me feel as if I was a burden in any way, but looking back, I know what a sacrifice it was for her and Sam. I remember always looking to find change in parking lots, vending machines, pay telephones, anywhere someone one might have dropped or forgotten to get their change, and when I gathered enough, Debbie would take me to Sonic for a ten-cent kiddie Coke.

Mama also seemed to be handling the loss in her own way, working long hours and staying out with friends. I cannot imagine all the pain she was struggling with, and I know staying busy must have helped her cope. She had work and her friends to keep her occupied, and she eventually married again.

My new dad was Merle. He was kind and generous, truly a good dad. Before he came along, I always had to walk to school, no matter what the weather was like. Merle felt that it was time for me to have a ride, so he took me to Yukon and bought me a brand-new straight-off-the showroom-floor 125 Yamaha Enduro motorcycle! Man, I was so proud of that thing. As a girl who had not had many material things throughout my life, this motorcycle was like getting a million bucks. I had something to call my own and a way to real freedom. I had wheels, and I was going to travel.

With my newfound freedom and rebellion rumbling inside, I was out on the town doing whatever I wanted with whomever I wanted. One place I loved to go to was the pool hall in Calumet, a town about fifteen miles away, and I would hang out there for hours. They had pool tables, shuffleboard, and game machines, and all the older men would come and play cards and dominoes. I met a cute older guy at the pool hall and convinced him to buy us beer. Those meetups at the pool hall became our regular thing, and my new older friend got used to me coming.

One day I came in, having a bad day, hurt and furious. Who do you think was right there, listening while I cried about my broken heart? Of course, it was my new friend. Wouldn't you know it? That "cute older guy" ended up being my first husband. He was twenty years old and I was fourteen when we started dating.

We dated a short time before he asked my mom if we could marry, and she said yes. I was fifteen years old at the time, and in Oklahoma, you could not marry at fifteen unless you were pregnant. I wasn't pregnant, so we drove down to Gainesville, Texas, and married on September 24, 1976. Ironically, eighteen months to the day that we married, my first child, Chasity Lynn, was born.

When we married so young, everyone assumed I was already pregnant, but I was determined not to get pregnant for at least nine months to prove I got married because I *wanted* to, not because I *had* to. Even though I was waiting at least nine months, I wanted a baby so much! I wanted to have something to love and someone who would love me back.

At first, my hopes and dreams came true because a baby does love you and need you, and the feeling of being a mother was amazing. Little by little, Chasity started to fill the hurt in my heart. But when you have deep trauma, no human love or relationship can ever be enough to make the hurt go away. The healing I received from motherhood was like tiny drops of water trying to put out a house fire; it just was not enough.

Even though I didn't know it, I was trying to do the impossible. I needed a love that was bigger and truer than any love I'd ever known. Getting married and having a baby would never fill that void. What I needed was a perfect love, a nonhuman love. I needed a Savior. I needed eyes to see my story in a new way, to take the broken pieces of my past and put them back together so that light could shine through. I needed a miracle.

It would not be long before I came to understand that God had been with me all along. He was carefully and gently leading me, delicately holding together my fragile and shattered heart. He was closer than I ever knew, but I didn't see it then. As I look back over my life, I see that God used others to rescue me. I saw *His* love in their eyes. I felt *His* tender touch through their care. When I look back, my story makes so much more sense. Looking behind me, I see God lining up the circumstances in my life for the redemptive part of my story. Until then, I'd only known an emptiness of the soul, but soon I would feel the freedom of God's love as He began to wash my pain away.

CHAPTER FOUR

My Rescue

When we married, we moved to Cleo Springs, Oklahoma, to be near his grandparents, Granddad Francis and Grammie. I loved being near them and helping with the family farm. This move felt like a huge boulder had been lifted off my shoulders; El Reno had symbolized darkness to me, and now I was in a new place. I was moving on, out of the home associated with the trauma of my past and on to a new chapter. I vowed to live far away from El Reno for the rest of my life, never looking back, leaving those hellish years in the dust.

I loved my new husband's family as my own, and they treated me like theirs. We were married so young and did not understand how hard it would be to make a relationship work. After four years, ours fell apart and we went our separate ways. Chasity was two years old by then, and she and I moved into an apartment in Fairview, Oklahoma.

I started flipping burgers at Queen's Kitchen, working double shifts just to pay the bills. Each morning I would take my baby to day care and head to work, with only enough time to pick her up before day care closed and take her to the evening babysitter's house before clocking back in at Queens. The restaurant closed at 9:00 p.m., and I would pick Chasity up to go home for a little sleep before starting all over again the next day.

I was always exhausted; money was tight, and I had very little time with the baby I loved so dearly. As the old saying goes, I was following in my mama's footsteps and could not imagine another way of life, but at the same time, I knew there had to be one. I'm a strong woman, a survivor, a go-getter, and always paying attention. These qualities were my saving grace.

One evening I was in the corner booth of a bar when I overheard some guys talking about starting an oil field company and saying that they needed a truck driver. Without hesitating, I walked right over to their table, introduced myself, and said, "I've never driven a truck in my life, but I can learn, and I need a job." One of the men, Ed Gifford, took my name and number, saying he would call me.

About two weeks later, I received that promised phone call with life-altering words on the other end: "Kathy, this is Ed. I bought you a truck in Oklahoma City, and we need to go get it."

In my disbelief, I could only reply, "I don't have a commercial driver's license." That was no deterrent for Ed, who told me we would take care of that by going over to Enid, where I could take the test.

I got off the phone feeling the overwhelming realization that this man had a lot of confidence in me and all I could really do was step up to the plate. Luckily, I perform well under pressure and I passed the test, commercial license in hand! We headed straight to Oklahoma City to get "my" truck.

The moment I laid eyes on it, I was both scared to death and thrilled about this new journey. The salesman walked out to the

lot and showed me every little detail on the truck—this bright red
Mack Truck with a chrome bulldog on the hood. I had stars in
my eyes when Ed turned to me and said, "It's your truck. Drive
it home." I will never forget climbing up into that driver's seat,
thinking I was on top of the world. After driving over two hours
to get back home, I knew how to shift the gears on that big rig and
it just felt right behind the wheel.

Hauling loads of dirt and rock and packing them with a D10
Caterpillar Dozer was my life now. My mind recalls the streak of
glowing headlights flashing by in the black night on the other side
of my windshield. The more loads I delivered, the more money I
made, which meant I was often driving three days straight before
stopping to sleep. But driving eighty miles an hour down the
interstate, hauling twenty tons of rock, was nothing compared to
the running I was doing from the load I carried inside.

Harder than ever before, I ran from the demons of my
childhood, spinning further out of control. I would drink whiskey
to fall asleep and then snort cocaine to stay awake for days on end. I
kept a fifth of Crown Royal in the cab of my truck and would drink
while on the road. I am so far removed from this way of life that
sometimes the memories feel like a movie playing on the big screen
of my mind, but this dangerous way of living was my actual life. I
have no doubt that God must have had an army of angels around
me, keeping my eighteen-wheeler on the road and keeping me from
killing myself or anyone driving near me.

My long hours on the road sometimes required that I take
Chasity with me to drive my route, and even talking about that
now, I am overwhelmed by God's grace to keep both of us safe.
We still lived in the apartment in Fairview, but the pay for my new
job was quite a bit more than I was making at Queens. I loved the
feeling of independence that came with making good money. I was

able to care for myself and my daughter, even making enough to have a little house built for us back in Cleo Springs, closer to family and Gifford Trucking.

Fairview and Cleo are only about ten miles apart, so even while we waited on the house to be finished, it was an easy commute. I do not know what I would have done during those years without the Foster family. I still loved them like my own, and they treated me like their biological granddaughter. It made being on the road not seem so bad, knowing that Chasity was safe and cared for either by Grammie or Great-Great Grandmother Lena.

Looking back at this time in my life, there is no question that God was doing things behind the scenes to get me to the place He needed to—a place where I was ready for Him. I was hard and strong on the outside, miserable on the inside, and exhausted with the path I was on. Of course, if you would have asked me, I might have told you I was more than fine making money, calling my own shots, partying and living it up, but I would have been deceiving myself.

Honestly, I had been lied to by the biggest deceiver for most of my life, and the lies and truth ran together like a river. I did not know what true love was and didn't trust anyone—I didn't need anyone but Chas and myself. When you've been living like an adult since before you were a teenager, life has a way of feeling upside down. But if you get quiet enough, you can see the nightmares, hear the demons, feel the loss of your innocence, and it's enough to make you feel that you're losing your mind. Therefore, I didn't stop long enough to think, because who wants to feel like that? Some of my childhood might have been stolen, but I would get over it. I was strong. You want me to act like a grown woman, that is what you'll get, and that's what I did.

For years, I played the game. I was whomever I needed to be to survive. I'd even tried to be a wife and part of a "normal family," but it didn't seem that was in the cards for me. Therefore, I numbed myself. I checked out with alcohol, drugs, relationships, money … anything to make me feel that I was in control. I thought that feeling numb was the same as feeling healthy, until there was a knock at my door.

Sweet Grandmother Lena had done more for me than I knew. Not only was she a safe place for my baby, but she had also stepped into the spiritual battle for us. She was praying for me and for my daughter. She loved God and believed with all her heart that He could rescue me from the destructive road I was on. She also loved her church and knew her community there would pray for me and love me too, so she invited them into our situation and asked them to pray for us.

Home from the road one evening, I was filling my time as I always did. I heard a knock on my front door and thought it was some of my buddies coming over to party with me. I couldn't have been more shocked to open the door and see Grandmother Lena's Methodist preacher, Charles Lynch, and his wife, Rosa Mae, standing there looking at me while I'd just been drinking and smoking weed. But nothing could have floored me more than their reason for coming by. "Can we pray for you?"

I might not have been a churchgoing gal anymore, but I knew enough to know that when a preacher shows up on your doorstep and asks to pray for you, you say yes. So I invited them in. I will never in a million years forget what came next, for it changed my entire life.

"We know how you're living your life, and it is wrong. But we love you and want you in church."

My jaw must have nearly hit the floor. *They knew how I was living, but they still loved me. They even wanted me in their church.*

25

My head was spinning. This was not how I remembered "church people" to be, but it felt *real*. They seemed *genuine*.

We sat down, and they spoke straight to my heart. Like slow motion, I could see images in my mind as they talked. I remembered kneeling by my bed to pray with Grandma Fannie Stass and the peace I felt when I looked at that picture of Jesus above my bed. Charles and Rosa Mae filled in all the details. Some I had heard before, but now it all made sense. It was like my eyes had been open for the first time—no more motion picture living; there was something real to live for. The truth came pouring out of their mouths, filling up the emptiness in my heart.

Jesus is the Son of God. He left heaven, came to Earth, and was born as a humble baby. He grew up in a small town in a simple family and lived His life with one purpose: to seek out and save those who were lost—the sick, the hurting, the sinners. I was every one of those things, and I was sick and tired of living that way.

I was ready for something to change, and I told them so. They immediately prayed with me, and I gave my heart and life to Jesus. The gentle face I had seen so many times when I looked at the painting above my childhood bed had now become my very own Savior, more meaningful and powerful than anything I had ever known. The seeds that my grandmother had planted in my heart as a child were now fully alive! Jesus has been there all along, but He is a gentleman and will not force Himself on you. He waits until you invite Him into your life.

Charles and Rosa Mae loved me, cared for me, and were patient with me. They mentored me, and that fact was huge because I believe this was the moment God began planting the seeds for what would eventually be the House of Healing. Of course, I didn't know it then. I only knew that I was a new creation; the old had gone and a "new me" was in its place.

Right there in my living room, I realized that God had protected me over and over throughout my life, and in that very moment, He did what I never would have dreamed possible. God freed me from addiction. I literally walked away from drug addiction, never looking back. That, my friend, is a *miracle*—the result of God's power and the prayers of some faithful grandmothers.

CHAPTER FIVE

My New Beginning

Oil field work tends to be a small world, which is exactly how I first heard the name Eugene Boeckman. He worked with people I knew, and I'd heard good things about his character, prompting me to see if he might have a need for a driver to haul rock.

Ironically, on September 26, 1982, at Dorothy's Bar, I had just been asking a friend to introduce me to Eugene, and he had heard about a driver who hauled crude oil and thought that driver was *me*. As he recalls, he walked into Dorothy's and saw this "beautiful blonde with dimples and blue eyes" playing pool. He walked up to meet me, we started talking, and he found out I hauled rock, not crude oil. However, that misunderstanding opened the door for us to become friends.

We talked awhile, and then Eugene walked me outside. A guy from the bar also followed me out and began harassing me. I gave him a verbal warning, but he kept coming at me. Because of my background, I can take care of myself, so I did. After the bartender broke up the fight, the guy told everyone that Eugene had jumped him in the parking lot, but the bartender set the story straight. When Eugene tells people about that moment, he says that that sealed it for him; he wanted to marry this beautiful feisty gal with blue eyes.

From that first meeting, we began spending more time together, playing pool and just hanging out. I was very gun-shy about getting into a relationship, having married and divorced so young, and I was not optimistic that it would be any different. So I kept Eugene at a distance, enjoying his friendship but not wanting to move forward.

I was also an incredibly busy single mom, working full time and spending my free time with Chasity. I didn't even have time to go to the Laundromat, so when my jeans got too dirty, I'd go out and buy a new pair. One night I was telling Eugene about all the laundry I needed to do, and he offered to do it for me. He laughs when he remembers that I had twenty-seven pairs of jeans alone, and with everything else, my clothes filled up *every* washing machine.

After that night, he said he'd never go to the Laundromat again … and he had a brand-new washer and dryer delivered to my house. I knew right then that this was a guy I wanted to keep around! To be honest, that kindness—doing my laundry *and* making sure I had a washer and dryer—was what caused me to realize that it was possible to have a man care for me. I was seeing love in *action*, and it felt safe. I opened my heart up to him, and we began dating in November.

EUGENE AND KATHY

On one of our most memorable dates, Eugene wanted to take me out to a nice dinner, followed by a concert. Not knowing I don't like seafood, he made a reservation at Red Lobster. I was trying to be polite, feeling like a fish out of water myself, but I ordered the seafood sampler. I tried one bite of a scallop, and it took everything in me to swallow the nasty thing down rather than spit it out. After that, I just pushed my food around my plate until he was finished, and then we headed to the Lloyd Noble Arena in Norman, Oklahoma.

The concert was a big country music star, Merle Haggard, whom we were so excited to hear. He had two lesser-known-at-that-time openers, a little redhead named Reba McEntire and a group called Alabama. Of course, both are famous now, but thirty-seven years ago, it was a different story.

The funny thing is, I had already met Reba at Queens Kitchen, back when I was flipping burgers. She had played at the Fairview

Rodeo and come in afterward with her band to eat. When I saw her, I wanted to get an autograph for my daughter, but Reba wouldn't do it. I decided immediately that I did not care much for her. Eugene, on the other hand, had posters of Reba on his wall. I did end up getting autographs from her whole band on the back of the order ticket, and I still have it to this day. It is a special memory because those same band members were tragically killed in a plane crash years later.

Our relationship continued to grow more serious, and we were engaged and then married on October 14, 1983. We were raised in different churches, so we compromised and had the wedding in the Catholic Church Eugene's family attended, with a Methodist minister, Charles Lynch, doing the ceremony. My then–five-year-old Chasity was our cute little flower girl.

WEDDING DAY

I will never forget when, a couple of months into marriage, walking down the hall toward the kitchen, where Eugene was frying sausage, I laid my head on the table and said, "I think I'm pregnant, because I can't handle the smell of that meat cooking!" When I found out I had a baby on the way, the alcohol was gone. I was again blessed with a beautiful baby girl.

Our daughter, Amber Dawn, was born on September 10, 1984, a month before our first anniversary. We lived in Cleo Springs in the little house I had built for Chasity and me and then moved only a couple of blocks away to a new house right before Amber was born.

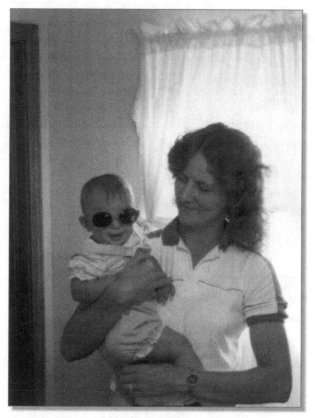

AMBER AND KATHY

Amber Dawn was and is the light of my life. Even though God had rescued me from drugs when I accepted Jesus, alcohol was an escape I still hung on to, but this tiny little soul had given me the courage to give it up. After the birth of Amber, I was finally getting my life together.

In all honesty, those early years were rough. I think we both went into it having no idea what marriage was all about. Eugene had never been married, my home growing up was so dysfunctional, and then the marriage from my teen years was also not what I wanted, so I had little knowledge of how to make marriage work.

With Eugene, I married a man raised completely opposite from my upbringing. He was from a strong Catholic family and was raised on a farm with eight siblings and parents who were still together. At twenty-six years old, he still lived at home to help with the farm, even though he also had a full-time job in the oil field.

I'm sure I was insecure, feeling as if his folks must have seen me as a girl from the other side of the tracks with baggage—a broken marriage and a child—but we were in love and Eugene was determined to marry me. I love the way he stood up for me and for our relationship. Over time, things smoothed out with his family, but it took years. The storms we have weathered have been hard, but cliché as it may sound, they have also made us stronger and given us the opportunity to help others.

Any red flags people might have seen from a distance rose up in full color once we were living under one roof. We had one child from the start, and adding another daughter with a severe case of colic made a tough transition even tougher. Our evenings were spent trying to calm the baby and get her to sleep. She would sleep about two hours and then wake up crying, at which point Eugene would buckle her into his truck and drive around checking wells while she slept. It was an exhausting time, to say the least.

But physical exhaustion was not our only enemy. Although I was a Christian at this point, I was still a new believer and had never seen what a godly marriage looked like or how to live it out day to day. To be honest, I also had some major theological questions brewing over how a loving God could have allowed the painful abuse in my past. But I was pushing away those thoughts, trying to plug into the most natural place when you want to learn more about God: church.

Eugene and I heard a statistic that 90 percent of kids who go to church with both parents will stay in church. We knew we wanted that to be part of our family, so because of our different backgrounds, he would get up and go to Mass and then come home to get us and our family would go to church together. We were involved at the church, serving in any way we could. Anything anyone needed—setting up tables or chairs, cleanup, helping with meals, teaching Sunday school—they called on us and we were there.

Although we are both naturally very service-minded, I would describe that season as "playing church." Not that we were being insincere by serving, but it was as though we hoped our marriage issues and past trauma would go away just by being active in our church. We were still being mentored by Charles and Rosa Mae Lynch, which I am forever thankful for. Honestly, I think being involved in church and having mentors kept our marriage together, *but* we desperately needed some healthy relationship tools to save our marriage, as we were crumbling at home.

I was especially crumbling inside, so wounded in my heart and mind. Childhood trauma will *never* heal by itself, and I had many scars that needed to be addressed. I thought my new husband would fix me, and I struggled with feeling as if I didn't deserve him. Even though he is a good man who truly wanted to care for me, there is only so much weight a person can bear, and I leaned on him way too much. It was like a tug-of-war in my head—I wanted to prove I was strong and independent and could take care of myself, but I also wanted to be loved and cared for by this man who made me feel so safe. I did not understand why my heart and mind didn't seem to be matching up.

Even in the safety of our marriage, the old darkness would peek through. For instance, Eugene is a tall, strapping man whose build reminded me of Roy's. If he would stand in the doorway of our bathroom or closet and talk to me while I was getting ready, I instantly felt trapped. I didn't know exactly what was happening. I wasn't conscious of the memories it was triggering; I just knew I felt ready to pounce. Of course, he didn't understand my sudden mood change, and I didn't know how to verbalize it. I sometimes still struggle with situations where I feel trapped, like riding in the back seat of a two-door car or on an airplane, but I have learned how to take control of my thoughts, take deep breaths, pray … and not lose it.

I also needed to learn the beauty of sexual intimacy within marriage. What God created to build a bond between husband and wife had been used by a sick man against me; what was sacred and special had been introduced to me as dirty and wrong. It would take time and counseling for me to begin to work through the demons of my past, and even the process of counseling made me feel ashamed.

When Eugene and I tried to talk through our marriage struggles with a counselor, I left feeling like the bad guy. I was the one coming in with childhood wounds, and as soon as the counselor heard the details, the session would turn to focus only on my past. It was true that my past needed healing, but we were there because our *marriage* needed help. It's a miracle we stayed together. I can tell you right now that we stayed because we *chose* (and still choose) to. We do love each other, and we have a redeemed story now, but these three decades have been far from easy. What you read here is a testimony of two flawed people determined not to give up on God or one another.

CHAPTER SIX

My College Degree

M y thirst for outlets to let off steam did not die down after marriage. I played on a softball team early on and loved the stress release of being on the field, smashing that ball. I remember that before one game, Eugene told me he'd give me a hundred dollars for every home run I could hit—it cost him six hundred dollars!

KATHY

Another competitive hobby I took on was race car driving. I raced in several races and even placed twice, in a 25-and a 200-lap enduro. The time behind that wheel felt fast and free, reckless but under control. I was growing older and more mature, but I didn't lose the feisty strong-willed spirit that I was born with.

KATHY (DRIVER) AND DEBBIE

When you are raised with very little and then work hard, climb the ladder, and begin to have something, it's easy to hold tightly to material possessions. Those things are like the physical evidence that you've "made it"; they are status symbols. It made me feel secure knowing that we had enough and were doing okay financially, but it created a false sense of security and control.

I especially loved nice cars—high-end sports cars were my babies, and I would treat them that way. I would spend time on Saturdays out on the driveway, hand washing my pride and joy, and you'd better not scratch one unless you wanted to see me come unglued.

Eugene is a natural giver, and he loves buying me things. I equated the gifts with his love for me, and I would work hard to be a good wife for him, trying to keep things "even." This kept us in a destructive cycle that can't be kept up because possessions don't last, and in a marriage, you are on the same team. When you start playing the game of trying to keep the score even, you are pitting one against the other. Marriage is about two people becoming one, and if one of you is trying to "win," you both lose. We needed help to learn how to love each other in healthy ways.

Even though I was able to earn a good living driving trucks, I never did earn a college degree. It was something I had dreamed of, so when Amber was about two years old and Chasity was eight, I went back to school to pursue a career in law enforcement. As you can imagine, with my background, this field seemed like a perfect fit. I had been on the other side of the law in small ways as a teen and had lived through horrific child crimes, so I wanted to work in a place where I could stop the "bad guys."

While in school, I began working in Major County as a jailer, then on to become a reserve deputy, in hopes that they would hire me full time after I graduated. The closer we got to May, the more I realized that was not going to happen in Cleo Springs. If I wanted to work in law enforcement, we would need to move to a bigger town, so we moved our family to Enid. I was able to work as a reserve deputy of Garfield County, then on to a paid position as a fingerprint expert, also serving arrest warrants. I partnered with our friend Scott, and we opened a private probation company called Stepping Stones to supervise adult offenders.

You have to understand the perseverance all of this took. School was never easy for me; it required everything in me to concentrate in class, recall the information, do the work, and take the tests. I was putting in all this effort for my classes while also raising the girls—and we also decided to be foster parents during this time. It was all a huge task. I don't mention this to brag or pat myself on the back, but I want you to know my story so you will understand that no matter what your setbacks, your past, your struggles or your hardships, if *I* can do these hard things, *you* can too. Don't let anyone or any circumstance make you think you can't.

PHYLLIS (MOM) AND KATHY AT COLLEGE GRADUATION

During this season, I also started going through counseling to try to heal my childhood wounds. We were still struggling in our marriage and needed help there, but I could not avoid the way my past was affecting my present. I was easily triggered by situations and events; I had anger that would explode when I was mad at Eugene, who hated conflict and would run the other way. Even our over-involvement at church was burning us out. We were trying to find favor with God and each other by our works. We couldn't say no when someone needed something and we were worn out … Then news came from Eugene's job in the oil field. We were being transferred to East Texas.

CHAPTER SEVEN

Home Sweet Home

What happens when you take a marriage that is already struggling and move the family far from home? The situation goes from bad to worse. It was 1998, and I had been working hard and enjoying my career for eight years back in Oklahoma. But now I no longer had my job to find fulfilment in, and Eugene worked long hours. Raising the girls without family, friends, or our church was beyond difficult.

We made it almost two years in Texas before I hit my limit. Right before school got out for the summer, I went to Eugene and said, "I've had enough. When school gets out, the girls and I are headed back to Oklahoma, with or without you." We truly were in a miserable place, and this was as close to over as our marriage had ever been.

Seeing the look in my eyes, knowing I was 100 percent serious, Eugene got on the phone with his company and asked if there were any job openings back home. The first response he got was not exactly what we were hoping for. Yes, he could come back to a lower-paying job, no company truck, and we would have to cover all expenses to move ourselves.

I'm sure he was discouraged, but I was so relieved that he was willing to move, so I got on the phone and asked our family to start praying! This was on a Friday, and the following Tuesday, we got a call from an engineer at the oil company, letting Eugene know that if he was interested, they had an assistant superintendent's position open for him, which included a raise and a company truck ... and they would pay to move us from Texas to Oklahoma. God is good! We were headed back home, and within three months, he was promoted to an executive level in the company.

KATHY, EUGENE, AND RYKER—HAPPY TO BE HOME

Back in Oklahoma in 2000, we were looking for a church. My mom and sister went to the same church where we went as kids. The same church where Roy sat in that choir loft staring straight through me while I sat terrified on the front row. There were so many dark memories at that church, and there was no way in the world I wanted to join, but I was happy to be back home, so I visited the church to be with my family.

As Eugene and I sat in the pew that first Sunday, I noticed a few youths smiling at me. We decided to come back again, and I began getting to know the kids. They were kids in need of adults to connect with, but the church did not have a youth minister. We started reaching out, and the kids instantly connected with us.

Eugene and I did all sorts of activities with that small group of teens. We encouraged them to serve others by visiting shut-ins and cleaning their yards or mowing the lawn, we laughed and talked while bowling, and we sparked adventure by taking them on a canoe trip. For us, this was not unusual; we both have hearts for serving others and want to make a difference in the lives of kids. We spent time with them and cared for them.

The pastor put a team together to start looking for a youth minister, and much to my shock, these teens went to him and said they wanted *me* to fill the job. The pastor contacted me and explained the situation asking if I would pray and consider becoming the youth minister. My immediate response: "No. I'm not smart enough or biblical enough, and I've never been in ministry."

I went home and told Eugene all about the conversation, and the Lord would not let it go. I thought about it constantly and felt true connection and concern for those kids. I finally went back to the pastor and said, "Okay, God is telling me I'm supposed to take this job. I may not feel qualified, but we can learn together."

My pastor just smiled and responded, "I knew you'd come back."

I began serving at the church, and kids were inviting their

friends. The group was growing, and it was exciting to be part of what God was doing in their lives. When I took the job, I thought it was for the kids—but God had His own work He was doing in me. As I look back on my story, this season is when *everything* changed.

For years, I had been pursuing healing through counseling. An especially helpful form of therapy was EFT, or emotionally focused therapy, which focuses on your adult relationships from the past, specifically those related to trauma. My therapist would guide me as we looked back at patterns in childhood relationships and the way those relationships were affecting my ability to attach and bond with others.

As we looked back and learned from my past, I could take steps to create more secure bonds and develop more trust in my current relationships. EFT helped me process the events of my childhood and the underlying anger I still felt. I am a firm believer in getting help from a doctor or Christian counselor and to this day will reach out to one when I am in a difficult season.

I was learning how to calm my body and mind when I felt anxious or triggered, and I could see a healthy change in my life and in my marriage. Being back in Oklahoma was good for us; even being back in the church of my childhood was proving to be okay. I was serving the Lord there, and life was busy with my own kids and the youth group, but God had more He wanted to show me. My tendency is to go full force and full speed and then move on to the next thing, but God had to bring me into *this church* that held so much darkness and *keep me there* for a period. Week after week, I was sitting in the pews, fighting the demons of my past.

God was calling me over and over to let go of those demons, to *forgive* my offender. This might not have happened if we had not landed in that church, and truth be told, I don't know if we would have stayed there had I not become the youth minister. By

God's grace, we stayed for the kids; by His grace we actually stayed for me.

The time back in that church redeemed my story. Yes, it had been filled with so much pain, but God was connecting the dots for me. *Because* of the pain of my past, *because* of the abuse I had experienced, I could understand and connect with teens who were hurting. My heart is drawn to justice and mercy; I can identify with trauma. I know the ache, the self-medicating, and the running. I can speak to these kids and love these kids *because* of my experience.

As I look back, I can see that God took me back to my very beginning for two specific reasons. First, to show me what it was like to serve Him, to be useful for His Kingdom, and to see that my past was incredibly helpful in ministry, not a hindrance. Second, He brought me to the point where I was truly able to forgive Roy. This is the most difficult thing I have ever done, but being in that place and seeing God make beauty from my brokenness, I couldn't hold onto unforgiveness any longer.

Let me be clear that forgiveness does not mean saying, "It's okay; it's no big deal." Sexual, physical, and verbal abuse is absolutely *not* okay, and it *is* a big deal. That type of trauma will leave wounds on us that only God can heal.

Then what *is* forgiveness? Psychologists generally define forgiveness as a conscious decision to *release* feelings of resentment or vengeance toward someone who has harmed you. Forgiveness does not depend on whether or not you *feel* as if they deserve it, and it certainly *doesn't* mean forgetting or excusing horrific offenses.

Honestly, forgiveness is for our own growth and peace, much more than for the other person. When we hold on to hurt, pain, resentment, and anger, it literally tears us up on the inside. Things like anxiety, stomach issues, panic attacks, sleeplessness, and other daily physical symptoms can all be traced back to unforgiveness. These feelings are hurting us rather than "getting even" with our offender. Nothing we can do will undo the past. Typically, the offender is unaware that we are suffering—they have moved on or maybe they are no longer living. Therefore, our unforgiveness is only hurting ourselves.

On the other hand, when we release the past and offer forgiveness, we become free to live in the present, to move on without anger, anxiety, or destructive habits. Please do not misunderstand me by thinking that this is a simple one-time step. The deeper the hurt, the more we will have to forgive, sometimes every hour, when we remember what was done to us. But the more we forgive and let go, the less power the past has over us, until eventually the memories are less frequent.

Jesus was once asked, "How many times should I forgive someone? Up to seven times?" The disciple asking the question chose the number seven because it symbolizes the perfect number, the number of completion.

Jesus surprised everyone who was listening by saying, "I tell you, not seven times, but seventy times seven." Jesus responded this way not to say that after four hundred and ninety times, we are done and will not need to forgive again. Instead, the point He is making goes back to the idea that seven is a perfect number. Rather than limiting our forgiveness to merely seven times, seventy times seven signifies eternity. Forgive others infinitely, just as God has forgiven us to eternity. If you want to read more about forgiveness, this story is found in the Bible, in Matthew chapter 18.

We will never have to forgive an infinite number of offenses, but the memories can feel never-ending. However, each time we remember the offense and are tempted to be sucked back into the anger and hurt, we have the opportunity to let it all go, forgive and trust God. This was the biggest lesson of my life.

We stayed at that church for about two years. I served the students as youth minister for about a year and a half, until the Lord then made it clear that He had somewhere else for us to go and continue growing. We started looking for a new church in 2002, and that is what led us to visit Council Road Baptist Church.

CHAPTER EIGHT

New Season of Growth and Training

W e attended Council Road a few Sundays and felt as if we were at home. We loved the teaching, and even though it was a larger church than we had ever attended, we decided to join. The very next week after we joined the church, the current pastor, Brother Mark, announced that the Lord was moving him to another church in Texas. I can promise you this was God's divine timing because had that announcement come one week earlier, we never would have joined. I had been in churches before when a pastor left and it was followed by dysfunction and a church split, and I wanted nothing to do with that kind of situation. I wanted a healthy, stable church home. But I am also a woman of my word, and since I'd already made a commitment to join the church, I decided to stay and see what would happen.

During the interim, we had a fantastic preacher named Anthony Jordan, and he kept us coming back, while the search team prayed for wisdom as to who would be Council Road's next pastor. In less than a year, we brought in a wonderful man who was currently leading a church in Texas but had been raised in Oklahoma, just down the street from our church. Rick Thompson became our pastor and brought with him a renewed heart for missions and the vision for getting this large church into smaller groups, where community and relationships can really happen.

After having a taste of serving in our previous churches, I knew I wanted to be involved in some capacity at Council Road. My only hesitation was the fact that Eugene still attended Mass at his Catholic church every Sunday before coming to church with me. This didn't bother me at all, but in the past, I had run into people who had an issue with that. True to my feisty self, I decided right up front that I would let our new pastor know our situation, honestly half expecting a disagreement.

One of the first weeks he was officially on staff, I marched into the pastor's office and told his secretary I wanted to meet with him. She kindly let me know that I needed to make an appointment and come back another time, but I did not take no for an answer. I was feeling bold and ready to confront this issue right off the bat, so I bolted right into Rick's office, taking him completely by surprise. I sat down, looked him square in the eyes, and said, "I need you to know something. My husband, Eugene, and I come as a team, but he attends both the Catholic Church and Council Road. Can we serve here together?"

Clearly a little stunned by our first meeting, Rick calmly looked back at me and said, "I don't have a problem with that at all." I felt my shoulders relax, and a smile came across my face as I shook hands with my new pastor and let him know how glad I was to have him at our church. This conversation was pivotal for me, and for *us*, for Eugene and I felt the freedom to serve together with our pastor's blessing. We had no idea what kind of ministry was in store for us, but within a few months of Rick's arrival, it became clear.

Along with introducing the importance of each member of the church getting connected to a smaller community group, our pastor brought before the staff the need for a program called Celebrate Recovery, a Christ-centered twelve-step recovery program for anyone struggling with hurts, habits, or hang-ups of any kind. One of our staff members was placed over the Celebrate Recovery (CR) ministries, and he put together a team to train and launch the ministry to the rest of the church. Eugene and I were asked to be part of the initial team, and it was instrumental, not only for those who would attend but also for us. What started as training to help others who were hurting led us to the tools we needed for health in our marriage. Not only that, but on a personal level, the remnants of pain I carried from my past were confronted as I worked through the twelve steps of CR for myself.

Our church invested in our team by taking us an hour and a half away, to Tulsa, to attend a CR meeting at a church there so we could see the ministry in action before we began leading our own groups. Once the ministry kicked off, our team also had the opportunity to go to Saddleback Church in Orange County, California, for more training.

After I returned from California, I once again felt a pull toward helping teens, so I began volunteering at Council Road's facility across the street, called the Cube. This building is open to the community for basketball and is just a safe place to hang out. I began connecting with some of the teens over there and started using the CR curriculum to lead them through the twelve steps for their own issues.

One of the requirements for those of us who were leaders in CR was to work through the steps on our own so that we could lead others to do the same. This process ended up having a powerful effect on our whole family. As Eugene and I went through the steps separately, both dealing with any issues that came to our minds and hearts, it took us all the way back to the basics. We recognized that there *is* a God and He is in control, not us. We began having deep conversations with each other about our personal walks with Christ.

Through our separate time going through the CR material and our talks together as a couple, the Lord worked in Eugene's heart to draw him closer to Him. As my husband describes it, up to this point, he had been riding on my coattail, spiritually speaking. When we served, we served together, but it was always wherever God was pointing me, and Eugene would serve and work behind the scenes. I moved over to work in Celebrate Recovery with teens, and the team asked Eugene if he would become a leader of a small group for adults. It took him by surprise, but he said yes, and one of our dear friends, Sue Ellen, said, "We knew you would do it; we'd been praying about you serving."

As Eugene was growing in his knowledge of the Bible and leading others, he knew God was calling him to be baptized. He had been baptized as a baby but wanted to make a public profession of what Christ has done in his life as an adult. It was a memorable David and Goliath kind of moment, with a few quiet laughs as our friend Dann, the shortest member of our staff, baptized my six-foot, six-inch husband.

The changes in us were affecting our home dynamic as well. I began to realize how controlling I had been, and in a men's Bible study called Men's Fraternity, Eugene recognized the need for him to lead our family. We began to read scripture together and grow in our faith, which truly saved our marriage. After years of issues under the surface, stress, and marital tension, God brought healing to us.

God was not only breaking my habit of control in my home; He was breaking the idol of materialism. Remember my obsession with sports cars and material things? All that changed one day when I raised the garage door and God placed in my heart a desire to give. I saw my beautiful 2002 Trans Am Collector Edition sitting in the garage and clearly heard God say, "Give it to the missions fund at church." At that time, CRBC was raising money to support the many mission's projects and partnerships the church supported, but Eugene and I didn't have any money set aside that we could give. However, I had my pride and joy and knew I needed to lay it at Jesus's feet, so I did. I donated the car to the church and was able to give more than I ever dreamed to the mission's fund.

I say this not to brag about the amount we were able to give but to testify to the idols God was breaking me free from one at a time. That step of faith made a huge shift in my thinking, and to this day, I no longer carry the burden of materialistic living. My heart and life were continuing to change, and I was filled with joy.

During this same time frame, we joined a Sunday morning class together and were building relationships with other believers. Our class had been praying for several months about a service project we could do together, and then the tsunami hit Sri Lanka in 2004. This was right around Christmas, and the leader of our class approached the group to see if there was any interest at all in an international trip. At the time, you couldn't go into the country as a missionary, but you could come in to help the community.

Pastor Rick knew some people already serving full time in Sri Lanka and was able to connect our group with them. We were told we could come in as a work crew to help with water wells and tsunami cleanup. This type of work was perfect for Eugene and me, but the timing seemed off. I had severely injured my neck, and we had been researching doctors locally and overseas to see where I could get the best treatment results. We knew procedures would be expensive and were not sure whether we should take the opportunity to go on an international mission trip or spend that money on my medical needs. We prayed that God would give us wisdom about how to spend our money and time.

I went back and forth on what we should do and finally one evening said, "Lord, you're gonna have to just tell me what to do." The next morning, when I got up to read my Bible, this verse jumped off the page as His answer to me: *For I am the Lord your God who takes hold of your right hand and says to you, Do not fear; I will help you* (Isaiah 41:13). As I read those words, I knew God was telling us to go on the mission trip and that He would take care of my body and the pain I had been in.

In July 2005, after months of planning and preparing, we took a life-changing trip with a group from our church, traveling 9,400 miles away to serve people who had literally lost everything. Eugene and I had never been this far from home. The flight alone was quite an experience! Traveling more than sixteen hours in the air while confined to a large airplane is enough to bring out more than a little claustrophobia, but what God did through that trip was worth the discomfort.

WATER-WELL RESTORATION TEAM—THANK YOU!

As we worked that week, God had two incredible blessings for me personally, not to mention the blessing we were able to be to the community we helped. First, I had zero neck issues the entire time we were there, and the work we did was extremely physical, enough so that I should have been in pain. Second, the Lord began to put a strong desire for missions on my heart. At first, I thought it was simply a response to being in another country, doing meaningful work, and wanting to re-create those feelings once we got back to the United States.

KATHY AND EUGENE WORKING HARD

However, weeks after we were home, the calling was still there, getting louder. I assumed God was telling us to sell everything and go on the mission field since that is where we were when I first started feeling the nudge in my spirit. I shared my ideas with Eugene, and to my surprise, he did not see the same vision. I was stunned and confused. Why was God not making this calling clear to my husband too?

I could not deny the pull toward missions, but it was too big of a decision to be impulsive, so I waited and asked God to speak to me. Around the same time, in downtown Oklahoma City, I attended a large conference called Women of Faith. A weekend full of powerful teaching from God's Word, worship, prayer, and encouragement from other women was exactly what I needed.

I will never forget one of the women speaking that weekend, sharing about the great need for adults to get involved in the lives of teens. Hmm ... that sounded familiar to me. I had always been drawn to helping teens—from foster care, to youth ministry, to the program Celebrate Recovery for teens—and this definitely seemed to be an area where I was gifted. The problem is, when something comes naturally to us (in other words, a God-given part of our personality), it feels less like ministry or something unique and more like how we are wired. Until this point, I had not thought too much about the fact that I kept being drawn back into ministries that supported teens. Even then, at the conference, it was not an aha moment as much as a small seed planted, connecting some of the dots of my life.

I went home from Women of Faith encouraged spiritually and chewing on all the different things I had learned from the women who taught that weekend. I was still waiting on God to show Eugene that we were supposed to move overseas, but I was also mulling over what that woman said about teens in need of healthy adult relationships. I did not need anyone to convince me of that—I had been one of those teens, and I knew the impact my mentors had made on me. So I started researching organizations that were already doing work with teens and stumbled upon a group from Florida doing some interesting work. As the Lord would have it, this group from Florida had a conference coming up.

I was seriously considering going to the conference but was also confused because it seemed pointless to do more research about ways to help teens when I had felt a call to missions in Sri Lanka. Only Eugene knew about these questions on my heart and mind at this point.

The Sunday before I would head to Florida for the conference, I was walking down the hall at church when one of my older and wiser godly friends, Jackie, stopped me. We chatted a bit, and I said to her, "Can I be honest with you?"

She answered, "Sure you can."

I began to tell her about how I was really struggling with what God wanted me to do.

She looked me right in the eye and said, "Kathy, you need to claim this promise: 'No eye has seen, no ear has heard, and no mind has conceived the things God has prepared for those who love him.' I hope that encourages you." We both had tears in our eyes, and I knew exactly what that promise from 1 Corinthians 2:9 was supposed to mean to me. The direction I was going—heading off to learn more about working with teens—was exactly the direction God wanted me to go, and He had things in store that my mind could not conceive.

This truth was confirmed almost immediately after my arrival at the conference. I had some time to myself before the speaker began the first session, so I went into the chapel alone and prayed for God to lead and guide me. I read scripture, sat in silence, and prepared my heart for whatever the speaker would teach. Wouldn't you know it? The first verse she used in her teaching was 1 Corinthians 2:9. I felt God's kindness as He connected the dots from my "hallway moment" with Jackie to this very moment at a conference in Florida, more than a dozen hours away from home.

CHAPTER NINE

The Making of
a Ministry

My head was full of information and my heart full of encouragement when I returned home from Florida. At the conference, I learned about a specific program used in their work with teens, and I came home armed with information and intrigued by what they were doing. I began to explore partnering with that group and bringing their program to Oklahoma. By this time, my heart was fully drawn to helping teens, and I began to consider using my passion somewhere other than foreign missions, yet I still was not convinced that God didn't want us to move overseas.

As I spent time looking back over my life, it made sense that God would use my pain to bring healing to others—but I wanted to make sure I was on the path He had for me, not a path I was creating for myself (I had done that enough, and it ended poorly). I went to the Lord in earnest prayer: "God, please show me if this is the direction you are leading me. Is this what you meant when you called me to missions?"

It was not an audible voice that anyone else could hear, but I heard the Lord clearly say, "Kathy, this is your mission field, right where you live, working with teens." I felt instant peace—something I hadn't felt in months as I was searching for God's calling for me.

As God brought the vision into focus, it made perfect sense. He is gracious, loving, and kind, never wasting our pain. He is able to bring beauty from ashes and redeem even the darkest past. If we open ourselves up to Him, He will show us plans that go beyond our wildest imaginations—just like the verse my friend shared with me that day in the church hallway.

The more I looked into the program I learned about in Florida, the more I realized it wasn't a perfect fit for us here in Oklahoma. However, being able to see what another organization was doing for teens in their community was just what I needed to get my creativity flowing. I knew the needs around me were huge. I had experience, and I had a vision that God was calling me to serve my community. What I needed now was some clarity about exactly what programs were in place to help teens in our area—specifically teen girls—and I needed a name for this God sized dream.

Not long after the Lord made it clear that my mission field was in my own backyard, I was spending the day with my granddaughter, Kylie. We were swimming and talking as I shared all that God had been doing in my life over the past few months. I told her the hopes and dreams I had for the young ladies who would come into the program that I was now beginning to imagine, and I mentioned that I needed a name for it. We continued to play and swim for a bit. Then Kylie looked at me and said, "Nana, I got it. It's House of Healing for the Teenage Soul." And that was that. I instantly knew that the Lord had put the name of our ministry into the mind of my own flesh and blood—my own granddaughter, whose soul I love so much.

HOUSE OF HEALING ENTRANCE

Once again, true to my personality, I did not allow my lack of knowledge or experience to stop me. I had heard good things about the juvenile judge from Canadian County, Judge Gary Miller, so I scheduled an appointment to meet with him. I assumed that since he worked with adolescents on a regular basis, he would know the programs that were effective in helping these teens and the resources available to their families. I shared a little of what was on my heart and then asked him what was being done to address these issues in our area. This conversation was pivotal, as he told me there was currently very little offered for teen girls but *plenty* of programs for teen boys. Bingo! The calling was becoming clearer with each step that I took.

Let me pause for a moment to point out a very important pattern. God did not give me the entire vision for what He was calling me to do all at once. He planted seeds in my heart, bringing circumstances together—from the emotional transformation that happened at our old church, to understanding parts of my past, to the mission trip, and finally the research He was using to lead me to His desired destination. He was working all along, but I needed to listen and respond. If He had given me the entire vision at once, it would have been overwhelming. If He had left me alone with all my questions, without continuing to speak to me, I would have become discouraged and given up. Instead, it was a divine partnership: His speaking to me, followed by my steps of obedience—some steps small, others huge.

Mine is not an isolated case. This *is* how God works in the lives of His children. Our stories and situations are different, but His desire to lead us to the path He has created for us is the same. Are you listening? Do you have the courage to obey? This, my friend, is a promise from God to you: *For we are God's masterpiece. He has created us in Christ Jesus, so we can do the good things he planned for us long ago* (Ephesians 2:10 NLT).

As I continued to research and explore where work was already being done to help teens in our area, the current children's pastor at our church was plugging in at Western Heights, a school near us. He asked if I wanted to join him in the work there, and of course, I jumped in. I knew it was not the long-term vision God put on my heart, but it was work with teens who needed a positive adult influence, and any experience would be helpful.

While working with the school, I created a program called Learn, Serve, Lead, focusing on three phases to help take a student from the classroom into the community as a successful, confident, and service-minded member of society. The three phases were designed to motivate teens to take the next step in determining their career path and helping them on the path to attain that goal. Our hope was to instill core values in the students, empowering them to impact the lives of others as they served in their own communities. Many of these students never had a mentor or positive adult role model encouraging them toward the future.

The "Learn" phase of the program encouraged the students to stay in school, graduate or get their GED, and continue their education in college or a trade school. Mentors connected with the students as tutors and life coaches, helping them to cope with peer pressure and daily life situations. We also held a mock job fair at the school, with businesspeople from the community conducting interviews with the students. This gave them a feel for how to dress and the questions they might be asked in an actual interview. The companies were often actively seeking employees and ready to make a job offer.

The "Serve" phase of the program was designed to help the students see the needs of the community and how they could step up to help meet those needs. Service projects, such as picking up trash around the school, volunteering at the food bank, or working at a Habitat for Humanity project, allowed the students to get involved in the community and showed them that *they* could make an impact. The students received the powerful life experience that it is truly more blessed to give than to receive.

The "Lead" phase of the program helped the students to dream of the life and career they wanted to pursue, giving them a sense of what it would take to accomplish it. Character building and behavior-based programs were used to help identify core values and to help the students adopt that lifestyle. Classroom activities were designed to teach the students to respect each other and the guests that came into the class. The instructors also modeled respect to the students, something that was normally missing in their lives. The program was incredibly beneficial in the lives of the students, and the experience was so valuable for me.

I remember mentoring one young woman who seriously needed a temporary place to stay. She was bouncing from friends' couch to couch because home was not a healthy option; she desperately needed support and stability. It was frustrating because I felt helpless as I looked at her situation, but it also confirmed the huge need for a *residential* home for girls in need of a fresh start—the very dream I had on my heart. More than anything, I wanted to see this dream become a reality, but there were so many steps to get from *A* to *Z*. As hard as it was to wait, knowing young ladies needed a home *right now*, I knew this vision would only be accomplished by taking one step at a time.

Eugene and I started looking for property where we could build our ministry as soon as we were able to get all the paperwork filed to make the House of Healing an incorporated nonprofit organization. We looked at several different setups, but each time we knew it was a closed door for one reason or another, and we were not able to finalize the purchase on any of the initial properties we pursued.

Back in 2006, before the House of Healing, the two of us purchased thirty-six acres of land to build our own home on. We were still living in Yukon at this point, but we were anxious to build and move out to the land. Two years later, we still needed to sell our current house in Yukon, but the contract fell through.

One day while we were out at the land, it hit us. Part of our thirty-six-acre property was perfect for House of Healing! After talking it over and driving around the land in our ATV, we decided to donate ten acres of our personal property to build HOH. We did have one little problem, though. At this time, there was not an accessible road to get over to where the House of Healing side of the property would be. There is a pond on the land, which makes the property beautiful, but it also made it too expensive to put a road in. We would need an easement, which would involve one of our neighbor's properties as well as ours.

We knew it was worth a try, so we contacted one of our neighbors, Ben McClain, and scheduled a meeting about getting an easement across his land in July of 2009. When we met with him, he told us he would rather sell the land than give an easement. He had seventy-two acres total and would not divide it up. House of Healing could only afford to purchase twenty-five acres, so Eugene and I purchased the remaining forty-seven acres. We were so excited to be moving forward with such big steps … The ministry had a home!

Later that year, in November, Ben reached out to us and explained that he was excited about the way we were going to use the land. He had been thinking about HOH, and he wanted to leave a legacy behind. He had kept a lifetime estate in the mineral rights but felt led to deed them to the House of Healing. Although we only bought twenty-five acres, we would receive about fifty-four acres of minerals. What a blessing!

After acquiring the land and finalizing the placement of where House of Healing would be, things started to take shape and really move forward. Our dream was becoming a reality! As a nonprofit 501(c)(3) organization, we began praying about who would serve as the House of Healing board of directors. The first board consisted of six members: four friends who supported our vision, Eugene, and me.

As the ministry developed, I was able to share my testimony and the HOH vision with different groups. Pastor Rick was extremely supportive from the beginning and helped me share my story. On a Sunday morning in worship, he showed a video of my testimony and the HOH vision, allowing our entire church to see what the Lord was doing. Through these opportunities at church, I met several like-hearted women who eventually became huge supporters of the HOH, using whatever gifts they had. We are so grateful for the people God brought alongside us (and He continues to bring people along!) because we could never accomplish this God-sized vision alone.

Paula Cummings is one of the women God has used in a major way. I met Paula in 2007, when I was sharing my testimony at an event. When I told my story, Paula remembers thinking, *I would love to be a part of something like that.* She approached me after I spoke and shared that she also had a passion for helping teen girls and would love to volunteer with House of Healing. At that point in time, the ministry was so new that I honestly didn't know what to do with volunteers, so I thanked her for her encouragement and told her I would be in touch if I found a spot where she could help.

Fast-forward about four years and I was sharing my story in a Sunday school class, which turned out to be the class Paula and her husband attended. They were in class that day, and she remembered me and the story of House of Healing. After class, she approached me again, asking if she could volunteer or help in any way. By this time, I had more organization around the ministry and knew where I needed people. I met Paula at her house to talk about HOH and that day asked her to be part of our board of directors. This was a new role for her, as she had typically served in youth ministry, teaching and discipling girls, but she was eager to serve in any way. Paula accepted the position and served on our board from 2011 through 2016. However, the biggest impact Paula made on HOH happened outside of the board meetings.

The more I got to know her, the more we connected, and she quickly became a sounding board for me, eventually becoming the program director. However, before we started developing the program, we were working hard raising funds. A major shift happened at our annual board retreat in 2013. I was still working with girls at Western Heights while working hard to build House of Healing. I was burning the candle at both ends and feeling extremely stressed out. At the retreat, I told the board I was stepping down from Western Heights so that I could fully focus on HOH as the executive director. The board pushed back, saying, "Kathy, you need to be working with girls. It's your passion." I was torn and confused. What they were saying made sense, but I was not physically able to juggle two separate ministries.

During a break, I went into the hallway to gather my thoughts. Paula followed me. As we talked, this question arose: "Can House of Healing start mentoring girls?" Asking it now sounds so funny because mentoring was always the vision of our ministry, but we had been so focused on fundraising that we had not been intentionally seeking out actual young ladies to work with. Standing there in the hallway together, we agreed. It was suddenly obvious: we *could* and *should* start actively mentoring young ladies. This had always been the sole purpose of HOH, and just as God would provide the funding, He would bring the girls who needed HOH.

Shortly after the retreat, Paula was driving down Kilpatrick Turnpike in Oklahoma City and had a picture in her head of the girls' ministry she used to lead at her church in Texas, followed by a picture of the Crisis Pregnancy Center where she had also volunteered. In that moment, the Lord gave her a crystal clear vision of the type of mentoring program that would work well at House of Healing.

She called me shortly after, excitedly telling me what the Lord had shown her and asking if we could try implementing the program. Of course, I said, "Go for it!" We reached out to several women as our first group of mentors and began to lead a small group of teens through the Authentic Beauty Bible study, by Leslie Ludy. We met at church for the study, along with mentors meeting one-on-one with the girls throughout the week. From this small beginning, we grew into year-round studies and mentoring, retreats and classes for parents, and a full equine program for the girls. Paula's impact on the overall ministry of HOH is beyond what words can describe—even our bunkhouse is marked by her.

A bunkhouse was first on our list of the physical buildings to save money for and build on the property. Eugene and I had asked an architect to draw up plans for a simple bunkhouse, a builder had given us a bid for the cost, and our board of directors had already voted in favor of moving forward. We were so excited that our plans were taking shape and we were close to breaking ground ... and then Paula called me.

She wanted to let me know that while she was spending time with the Lord, He had given her a vision for the bunkhouse that she would love to share with me. Honestly, I did not take that first conversation seriously because it seemed too late in the game to make a major change. But as a couple of days went by, I could not let the conversation go and told Eugene we needed to meet with Paula to hear what she had to say.

We scheduled dinner with Paula and her husband, Chad,

within the next day or two, and Paula drew on a napkin the vision she had seen in her mind of our bunkhouse. What she saw in the vision was a large bunk room, a big bathroom, a spacious kitchen and pantry area, a living room, and offices. It was bigger and more detailed than our original bunkhouse plans, and we knew it would also be more expensive.

However, as Eugene and I talked after dinner, we both felt as if we should at least explore the option. The first step was to talk to an architect about drawing up new plans and then get a quote from our builder. After getting a bid, we would know the extra cost and could present the new information to our board. One value we have always held for House of Healing is to operate debt-free, only starting building projects once we had the funding for them. The extra cost of the bigger bunkhouse might just be too much for us, but we would at least consider it.

The first meeting with our architect went well, and he agreed to draw up the plans of the new design for a thousand dollars. Then we could take them to the builder of our choice. The price seemed fair, and we needed actual plans to get an accurate bid on the potential new building. The architect drew up the plans, we paid him a thousand dollars, and we took them to our builder to get a bid.

That very weekend, the father of one of our board members was getting married and asked to use the outdoor chapel on HOH property. Of course, we agreed and were honored for them to be married there. After the wedding, the couple handed us an envelope with a thank-you card and a one-thousand-dollar check! Right there on the property, God gave us back the exact amount we had just invested in the new bunkhouse plans. It felt like a direct gift from Him and confirmation that we were on the right track.

OUTDOOR CHAPEL

The board approved the new design and added expense, which would be around thirty thousand dollars. As we prayed for funding for the bunkhouse, God had another gift for us. Ben McClain, the gentleman we bought the land from, was so impressed with the vision of the House of Healing that he deeded the mineral rights to us as his legacy gift. We were contacted to lease the minerals to an oil company—and guess how much that was worth. Thirty thousand dollars! God is the God who aligns our circumstances and provides all that we need right when we need it.

In August of 2015, we broke ground on the bunkhouse, and it was completed in 2016. This was *finally* the beginning of establishing and growing programs to reach teen girls. House of Healing empowers teenage girls to take charge of their lives and become responsible, contributing adults in three specific ways: The Authentic Girl Mentoring Program, Tools for Change, and the Equine Experience.

BUNKHOUSE

The Authentic Girl Mentoring Program is designed to create a positive setting that instills values and confidence in each girl. We believe that through a strong mentoring program, teenage girls can receive the early intervention that results in better life outcomes. Teenage girls who are part of a mentoring program build the self-assurance and standards they need to overcome a negative social environment.

Tools for Change is a six- to eight-week training course for families who are struggling with parenting concerns. When a teenage girl has a healthy relationship with her parents, it creates a nurturing environment that gives her the courage to make good choices. *Supporting parents and establishing healthy families is the cornerstone of our programs.*

Equine Experience allows girls to interact with horses. Working with the horses has not only brought so much healing to the girls but also introduced new girls to HOH, who otherwise would not have found us. Working with horses is a powerful way for teenage girls to gain a deeper insight into their own feelings.

Horses are intuitive animals. As prey animals, horses have a developed keen awareness of their surroundings to stay safe. Horses are especially adept at reading humans—they will mirror not just our behavior but also our moods, feelings, and insecurities. They will also reflect confidence, quietness, and trust. Based on a person's posture, body language, and approach, horses can discern how much they can trust an individual. A horse will obey commands when it knows it can trust the trainer.

It is the horse's amazing intuitiveness that brings to light any insecurities or strengths a girl may have. Girls are usually initially excited to ride the horses, but when it comes time to lead a horse and work close-up, the girls are sometimes intimidated. If a teenage girl has a hard time trusting, communicates poorly, gets easily upset or frustrated, lacks confidence, or does not follow instructions well, it will come out during the session. The power of the House of Healing Equine Experience is that horses give instant feedback by mirroring our emotions. Girls can see how their negative feelings and emotions disrupt others around them.

Horses come in with no preconceived ideas about a person.

Girls might see others having success during the lesson while they are not. By asking *why*, we help them understand how their own behavior is causing a negative impact on the situation. When girls find success working with the horses, they experience a trusting partnership and see firsthand that this is the best way to obtain optimal results.

Most kids, especially teenage girls, want to follow the crowd. This behavior often leads to a diminished sense of identity, confidence, and self-worth. When this happens, some girls pull inward to hide their wounds and pain; others push outward in anger. Working with horses helps girls on both ends of the spectrum as well as those dealing with varying issues in between. As a result, we typically see a dramatic improvement in behavior, communication skills, trust, and confidence from the girls who participate in our program.

We have now partnered with public and alternative schools, allowing girls to come out to the arena during the school day to work with the horses and our mentors. It is *truly* mind-blowing what God has done through this particular program.

As I look out across the grounds of House of Healing, I'm overcome with gratitude for all that God has done. I see young women on horseback learning to trust and allowing God to begin healing the places of brokenness in them. I see the bunkhouse and outdoor chapel where countless hours of training, prayer, and growth have already happened; and I believe many more will experience change in these sacred spaces. I see the new covered arena where we can now run the Equine Experience year-round, regardless of weather. I remember the promise of God, spoken by my friend in the hallway at church, and I see with my own eyes what happens when God does more than you ever could dream or imagine.

SADDLE UP

A red bird lands on the fence in front of me, and I feel God's presence. The red bird has become a sign of God's healing in my own life. The color red reminds me of the blood of Christ, which He shed for us on the cross. Every time I see a red bird, I am reminded of God's guidance and protection in my life and His protection over the House of Healing. He led me and protected me all of my days—even throughout the terrible seasons—and I know that God is good.

The sovereign God is the *only one* who could take all the brokenness in my past and use it as a springboard to bring healing to so many others. The dark, ugly shattered places in my past have been beautifully brought back together. The scars are still there—and that's okay because scars remind us of where we have been and how far we have come. Scars are wounds that have been healed; they do not sting anymore because there has been new growth. I will always be grateful for my past. Would I wish it on anyone or want to do it all again? Of course not! Childhood abuse is a sick, twisted, evil scheme of the devil, not the way God intended. But my past was not wasted; my past is not my enemy.

I have come too far to let the pain of my childhood keep my mouth closed. I will not let Satan win by keeping the struggle to myself. When we share our stories of hope, lives are changed and God is glorified.

In the book of Revelation chapter 12, verse 11, in the Bible, it says that we have *two* ways we can overcome the enemy. First, by the blood of Jesus, which has already been shed for us. When He died, he was a sacrifice which covered all our sin—past, present and future. If we choose to accept Jesus, we exchange His perfect life for our imperfect one; He covers our lives with His righteousness, and *nothing* we can do will reverse that.

Second, we overcome Satan by the *word* of our testimony. When we open our mouths and tell the world what God has done for us, the enemy is silenced! Satan cannot stand in the presence of truth, and our testimony is the truth about what God has done to redeem our broken lives. God can take the worst things in life and use them for good so that the enemy does not have the last word about your life. Jesus does.

You might be wondering if I ever felt inadequate or struggled with my past after God started using my story for His good plan. The answer is yes. The enemy would like for me to feel used and less-than, but I know the truth. It is a battle much less often these days, but I do remind myself of who I am because of Jesus. In fact, one day when I was feeling especially low, the Holy Spirit put it on my heart to type out and print off who I *truly* am so that I can see it, read it, and walk in it.

This is who I am in Jesus Christ, my Savior. By His grace and with confidence and gratitude, I walk with the Lord daily, utilizing these gifts given to me by my Lord and Savior and enhanced by the power of the Holy Spirit.

I am:

Courageous

A mighty warrior of God

A fearless leader

An effective speaker

Forgiven

Triumphant

A mentor of young minds

A compassionate healer of the brokenhearted

An unstoppable mission accomplisher

A positive thinker

A master mediator

A skillful fundraiser

An energetic nana

A wife of biblical stature

A friend to the friendless

My stained glass story has been redeemed by Jesus and is being used for God's glory to show that all things are possible for those who love God and surrender to His uniquely beautiful plan for their lives. Will you let Him redeem your story too?

If you are looking for a life with meaning, a life with Jesus, nothing would make me happier than for you to reach out to Him. You can pray anything your heart feels—He hears you; He wants you to know Him personally. If you want to give your life to Jesus, tell Him today. He is waiting for you—just as he was waiting for me the day Charles and Rosa Mae came to my door. You can pray something like this: "Jesus, I believe that you are the Son of God who died on a cross for all sin and rose from the dead. I know I have sinned in my life, and I ask you to forgive me. Please wash me clean and make me new. I want you to be the Lord of my life; I want to follow you. I want to be a child of God. In Jesus's name I pray, amen."

The Bible promises that if you confess with your mouth that Jesus is the Lord and believe in your heart that God raised Him from the dead, *you will* be saved (read Romans 10:9). The Bible also promises that if you confess your sins, God is faithful to forgive you of *all* sin and cleanse you of *all* unclean acts (read 1 John 1:9). If you prayed a prayer like the one above, you are a *new creation*; you are a Christian. *Welcome to the family of God!*

Please reach out to us via our contact information at the end of this book. The reason the House of Healing exists is to point others to Jesus, and we want to be here for you to love you, encourage you, and help you grow stronger in your new faith.

CHAPTER TEN

Stories of Healing

As I look out over the property, stories of healing flood my mind. I see the faces of countless young women we have been able to serve. Each one has a different story, a different reason for partnering with HOH. We help teen girls who are at the end of their rope, girls looking for a mentor, families in need of relationship skills, girls looking for a major life change, and anything in between. I am humbled for all that God has done through our program.

I think of a young lady who lived with her dad and brother, always moving around because her dad couldn't stay in one place. She and her brother would have different "moms" in and out of the home regularly, and Dad would leave them home alone to go to parties or have parties at their house, right in front of them. Because of this reckless lifestyle, the kids were put in harm's way.

She was raped when she should have been protected—her dad was partying, and other family members who were there were drinking and negligent of her protection. She was in an extremely hard place, made to grow up before any child should. She was often left responsible to care for four or five children at a time, while she was only an eight-year-old herself.

When her aunt saw that she was living without food, water, or a clean environment, she took her in. She tried to help her precious niece work through the trauma of her past by taking her to therapy, but at that time in her life, it was not effective. Then her aunt heard about the House of Healing and knew they needed to try the program. The girl had always loved horses and being outdoors, but even still, she did not want to try House of Healing. She eventually figured that maybe she could just sit back and play with the horses, not participating in the sessions.

However, as the year went on, she had a breakthrough! She grew in her relationship with God, formed bonds with the other girls, and learned from the mentors, who helped her become the young woman she is today. As they do with all the young ladies, the HOH mentors loved her just as she was, mistakes and all. Something she took away from the program is the truth that we do not choose certain painful things in our lives, but we *can choose* to make the best out of our circumstances and become stronger as a result. She now understands that she does not have to be the person she was when she came to the HOH and that she can use her story to help other girls.

I remember our very first group Bible study around the table and see the face of one young woman. She lived in a stable home with both parents and her siblings, and she came to House of Healing looking for a mentor and group of girls with whom to learn and grow. Her relationship with her parents was difficult, but her mentor helped tremendously by talking through everyday issues and just spending time with her.

She began to open up to her mentor, developing a true friendship, and her behavior at home changed because of the tools she learned from the House of Healing, which impacted every area of her life. She participated in the weekly group meetings, one-on-one mentor time, and the annual retreats, all pouring truth into her when she was at an impressionable age. She has since graduated from high school and plans to attend college, one day helping others the way she was helped as a teen. The relationship with her mentor continues to be important to her, as do the relationships with the friends she made in their Bible study group.

I look over toward the stable and see the face of another young lady, one of our girls who came to the mentoring program at the age of twelve. She loved being outdoors among the trees and being involved in the mentoring program, specifically the Equine Experience. She came to HOH when her mom heard about it and brought her out with a friend. Her family unit is healthy, and she lives with both parents and her sister.

When her mom talks about the program and the impact it has had on her daughter, she says the biggest difference it made was in her self-confidence. She now stands up for herself and reaches out to others without being intimidated. She knows she has something to offer to the world, and now she has the tools to go out and impact the world around her.

She has seen that joy comes from Christ, not situations in life; happiness and joy are two different things. She feels joy when she is outdoors in nature working with the horses as well as learning about God from the mentors.

Another face I can picture is that of a sweet-spirited young woman. I remember the way God brought her to our program in a divine way, involving my friend Heather. Ten years ago, Heather heard me speak in her Sunday morning class and felt God leading her to contact me about organizing a 5K and 10K run as an HOH fundraiser. Although she had never done anything like this, Heather knew she wanted to jump in and help raise funds for our program. Of course, I was thrilled and said, "Yes, please!" To date, this race has allowed the House of Healing to raise over $75,000.

A couple of years ago, as we were gearing up for the race, a grandmother was looking at the newspaper and saw an ad for an upcoming fundraiser, The Easter Run: Benefiting the House of Healing for Teenage Girls. She immediately looked up the website for HOH because her granddaughter had recently come to live with them. Her granddaughter's homelife was not safe and stable, and she was beginning to make unhealthy choices and struggling in school. Living with her grandparents, getting a fresh start in a new school, and beginning to see a counselor were already making a positive difference in her life, and then they found the House of Healing.

She fell in love with the equine program and connected with the mentors. When her grandmother talks about the difference she sees in her granddaughter, tears fill her eyes and she explain it is a night and day difference. She knows God led her and her husband to move their granddaughter to their home for a fresh start. And she has no doubt that God led her to pick up the newspaper and see the ad for the annual race, connecting her to the House of Healing.

I remember one of the very first girls I mentored. When I met her, she was lost, lonely, and had no clue what to do with her life. In high school, she had terrible grades, hung out with kids who did drugs, and really did not care where she might end up. One of the first things I sensed when we met during her junior year of high school was the anger—she was mad for so many reasons, needing to forgive so much, and I could fully relate to her.

She had been put in a class with other "troubled teens," which is how we were connected. From her perspective, she had seen people come in and out trying to help the students, but what stuck with her was that I remained around. I kept coming back to her class week after week to hang out and talk to the students. I recall that she did everything possible *not* to talk to me that first year, but later she told me, "It was hard to avoid someone who truly cared about me."

She began to trust me, and I began to mentor her. I know at the beginning I saw more potential in her than she saw in herself, and I tried to help her believe that she could do so much with her life. We built a two-way trusted relationship. I walked into "her world," never judged her, and always loved her for who she was. She is a grown woman and a wonderful mom now, so different from the teen girl I met, with a heart to help young women just as she was helped.

I see another face as I reminisce about the young ladies we have been honored to serve. This girl came from a very difficult homelife. She felt her mom was not there for her, her dad abandoned her, and her stepdad abused her in many ways. Because of the unstable adults in her life, she had built up resentment and carried many burdens—she did not trust adults. When she came to House of Healing, she was hurting, burdened, and struggling, yet she was drawn to the Equine Experience.

As a result of receiving truth, love, and grace from the mentors, she found faith in Jesus Christ. She has developed self-esteem, and confidence has grown in her relationship with God. She recognized the need to let go of the heavy burdens she carried, and her life is so much freer.

It utterly amazes me how working with the horses paves the way to trust others again, but we continue to see the connection; she is just one example of the impact horses make on the human soul. She also struggled in school, but with the investment of HOH mentors in her life, she has grown in every area. She finished high school and received a full scholarship to play softball at a university.

My mind is filled with conversations from the past, with both girls and their moms who have found hope and healing in our program. I sat with a young lady on the porch of our bunkhouse while she shared with me the way she was now free from guilt and shame because of HOH and the way her mentor had inspired her … The smile on her face was contagious.

Another teen in our Equine Experience told me that before coming into the program, she was not able to open up and talk to her mother; the relationship was strained. After learning communication tools, she has now grown in her relationship with her mom, and their communication is healthy.

Another young woman attended one of our retreats and shared with me that she came face-to-face with the reality of what she had been basing her value on. She was able to see that her focus had been on whether or not she was pretty, creating a low self-image and negative choices. After lessons learned through mentoring, she now understands that it is what's on the inside that matters most and that all of us are made uniquely beautiful.

One day I received a phone call from one of the moms, telling me how thankful she was for HOH. She admitted that raising a teen girl today is so difficult but that she has gained confidence and tools to help guide her daughter in the right direction.

A teacher from one of the schools we partnered with spoke at our annual fundraising gala and shared personal letters from some of the girls in her class who were a part of the Equine Experience program. She was teary-eyed, and my own eyes filled with tears as we heard words of renewed hope from girls who felt they had little to offer the world and little confidence in their futures before coming into our program. I hope you hear me when I say that this is the work of God, not me or anyone else in our program … Only God can change lives and write new stories for the broken.

Tears begin to form as I remember precious faces from the

past ... and I am filled with hope for faces I haven't met. It has been a long journey getting to this place, yet I feel more hopeful than ever about the doors the Lord will open.

As you can see, there isn't a girl who can't benefit from our program. We are here for girls at any place in life. We believe that every teen girl needs a mentor, but some are in more desperate situations than others are. The girls in harm's way are the ones who keep us up at night, praying for a way to bring safety and stability to them while introducing them to the rescue of God. Some of these girls need weekly mentoring and involvement in the program, while others need a safe place to live.

We are working toward getting our first home opened, fulfilling the very first vision God placed on my heart. Proverbs 24:3-4 says, "By wisdom a house is built, and through understanding it is established; through knowledge its rooms are filled with rare and beautiful treasures." We are confident that God will fill HOH with those rare and beautiful treasures, which are the teen girls who will reside within the walls; and through *His* wisdom, it will be established.

Our programs and partnerships continue to grow as we build connections with local schools. The Equine Experience has far exceeded my imagination, as we have seen the impact working with horses has on emotional healing. We average eighty-five girls each year, working through our program and gaining confidence, life skills, and so much more—impacting their families, schools, and communities. To date, we have served over five hundred families, since opening the doors to the House of Healing. Our Tools for Change program is changing the fabrics of families, creating new patterns and healthy communication for a lifelong generational impact.

The Lord continues to take the feeble dreams in my heart

and make them a reality. For example, this book is an answer to a vision the Lord put on my heart years ago. I had a picture in my mind of every girl who walked into our program being able to take my story with them, literally, in hopes that they would have hope in the God who could make their broken journey a beautiful story. I want them to take my story and read it when they need hope and pass it on when they meet another young woman who needs hope.

I also plan to give a handmade quilt and a stuffed animal to each girl who stays in our residential home, giving them tangible items to cling to, hopefully as they begin to cling to God. He has been the source of everything in my life. Isaiah 50:7 is the truth of my life and story: "Because the Sovereign Lord helps me, I will not be disgraced. Therefore, I have set my face like flint, I know I will not be put to shame." I know I had no control over my circumstances and looking back I think of how the heart of my heavenly Father was breaking for me. Thankfully, His plans were greater than any man could take away from me and my journey led me to victory in Christ.

Many people have asked me, "What is House of Healing?" Simply put, House of Healing is a nonprofit Christ-centered home that provides a safe environment where young women ages thirteen to seventeen can experience unconditional love, acceptance, and restoration. We work closely with the girls to help them find healing emotionally, physically, and spiritually and to educate, support, and guide them into a bright future. We also work with families, offering biblical counseling, training, and discipline techniques to reconcile and restore the family unit. In our program, teens gain skills that will equip them to live productive lives within their communities. In a word, House of Healing is a *lifeline*.

MAKING AN IMPACT!

As you can see, the opportunities are out there, the mentors ready and the horses waiting. Do you know a teen girl who needs to be connected to House of Healing? Are you interested in partnering with us?

For more information or to be connected to our program, contact us at https://www.house-of-healing.org/contact.

ACKNOWLEDGMENTS

I believe in miracles because I am one! There is absolutely no doubt that God had His hand of protection on me when I was making some very unhealthy choices. Not only did He protect me from my own craziness, but He also placed people and programs in my life at the perfect time.

Primarily, he gave me my best friend. Eugene has been my rock. He is patient, kind, and generous of heart. He has stood beside me through the good, bad, and ugly moments of living life with an adult who has not dealt with a traumatic past. Thank you for choosing to forgive and help in my healing process. You are my hero!

To my beautiful daughters, Chasity and Amber, I am extremely proud of you and grateful that I get to be your mom. Thank you for your love and kindness.

To my five beautiful grandkids, you have a special place in my heart and will forever be my pride and joy. Love you bunches!

To some very special friends who have prayed and encouraged me through this journey—Jackie, Karen, Vicki, Nancy, Paula, Amy, Angie, Olivia, Stacee, Clint, and Deb—you have lifted me when I was weary and ready to give up. For you, my friends, I will forever be grateful!

To Heather McAnear for putting words to my voice and

making this dream of sharing my journey a reality. Thank you is not enough to express my appreciation and love for you!

To all the volunteers who have given of their time, thank you!

Lastly, to the precious donors who truly grasp the vision of House of Healing and have given their hard-earned dollars, *thank you* is not enough to express my gratitude for helping to make this dream a reality.

MEET THE HOUSE OF
HEALING FOUNDERS

Kathy and Eugene Boeckman founded house of healing from a passion to strengthen families and to invest in the lives of teenage girls

Our programs are designed to help families bond close together whether they are already on the right path or need support to get back on track.

At the core of our mission is to provide teenage girls with a positive experience through our mentoring and equine programs to instill in them the right values to make positive life choices.

~Kathy Boeckman

We have seen so much growth in our programs, thanks to the support from our donors and volunteers. I am excited about our future and the many more families whose lives will be touched by this ministry. We now have girls who were teenagers a few years ago come back to serve and mentor others.

~Eugene Boeckman

EUGENE AND KATHY BOECKMAN

ABOUT THE AUTHOR

Kathy is a survivor of childhood abuse and broken relationships, yet God has done more than she could have ever imagined because of her journey. Through the power of God, Kathy was able to finally forgive her childhood abuser, move forward in health, and now helps countless young woman pursue their own freedom and healing from brokenness. The House of Healing offers multiple programs including: Authentic Girl Mentoring, Tools for Change and Equine Experience, all with the goal of helping young ladies find healing from the past, the tools to live a healthy life today, and a vision for their future potential.

For more information about House of Healing visit: www. house-of-healing.org

Printed in the United States
by Baker & Taylor Publisher Services